Healthy Lifestyles

BALANCING WORK AND PLAY

Camilla de la Bédoyère

amicus
mankato, minnesota

This book has been published in cooperation with Evans Publishing Group.

© Evans Brothers Limited 2010
This edition published under license from Evans Brothers Limited.

Published in the United States by
Amicus
P.O. Box 1329, Mankato, Minnesota 56002

Printed in China by Midas Printing International Ltd

Library of Congress Cataloging-in-Publication Data

De la Bédoyère, Camilla.
  Balancing work & play / Camilla de la Bédoyère.
     p. cm. -- (Healthy lifestyles)
  Includes index.
  Summary: "Discusses the importance of and gives tips for managing stress in your teenage years to achieve a balance between studies, jobs, family and friends, hobbies, and other leisure activities."--Provided by publisher.
  ISBN 978-1-60753-083-1 (library binding)
 1. Work--Juvenile literature. 2. Leisure--Juvenile literature. I. Title.
  HD4902.5.D45 2011
  650.1--dc22

                    2009047569

Picture Credits
Alamy: 9 (Gabe Palmer), 11 (Greg Vote), 12 (Adrian Sherratt), 17 (Janine Wiedel Photolibrary), 21r (SHOUT), 27b (Photofusion Picture Library), 30 (Bubbles Photolibrary), 31 (Aflo Foto Agency), 32 (Helene Rogers), 34t (Jupiterimages/Comstock), 39 (Mark Phillips), 43 (Bubbles Photolibrary); **AP Images:** 23; **Corbis:** 19 (Ariel Skelley), 24 (Creasource), 28 (Image Source), 33 (Scott Houston/Sygma); **Dreamstime:** 7 (Franz Pfluegl), 10t (Monkey Business Images), 21b (Radu Razvan), 29 (Val Thoermer); **Fotolia:** 10b (Marek), 27r (Darren Green), 41r (JenKedCo); **Getty Images:** 13 (Bruce Laurance), 36 (Ian Shaw); **iStock:** 6-7 (Skynesher), 14 (John Gaylord), 15 (David H. Lewis), 20 (Pali Rao), 22t (Tom de Bruyne), 25 (Frans Dekkers), 26l (Michael Krinke), 37 (Sean Locke), 38 (Chris Schmidt), 40 (Stock Photo NYC), 41l (Randolph Pamphrey), 42 (Kurt Gordon); **Science Photo Library:** 16 (Hank Morgan); **Shutterstock:** 18 (Yuri Arcurs), 22b (Ilya Genkin), 34b (Nicole Weiss), 35 (Trevor Goodwin).
Artwork by Graham Rich

05 10
PO 1560

9 8 7 6 5 4 3 2 1

Contents

Introduction

You are the sum of all your parts. This means that the genes you got from your parents, the environment in which you live, and the experiences you've had all contribute to this perfect blend of a person—you.

Who Are You?

As a child, adults made most of the big decisions about what would happen to you. As you move toward adulthood, however, you begin to share in the responsibility for those decisions. This can be a tricky time. There are so many things going on around you and so many people to please—including family, teachers, and friends. The challenge you face is to clear a path through the maze of work and play, obligations, and distractions. Choosing to manage your life puts you in charge.

A Perfect Balance

If you were asked to list the activities you need to do or like to do, they would probably fall into two main groups: work and play.

Work includes school studies, paid employment, and chores or responsibilities you have around the home. Work is something you may sometimes enjoy doing, but it's also likely to be something you *have* to do. Work usually offers important benefits—such as earning money, learning new skills, and career opportunities.

DID YOU KNOW?

According to young people, three of the most stressful—and important—issues they need to deal with are exams, bullying, and family breakups.

Play includes hobbies, socializing, sports, or just relaxing at home. Play is probably something you want to do, but it is just as important to your well-being as work, allowing you to exercise and enjoy new experiences.

Equilibrium means balance. When you have equilibrium in your life, it means you have the perfect balance between work and play. This balance can be hard to achieve, but we are getting better at understanding how important it is to find time to organize our lives, to get the most from our valuable time, and keep both our bodies and minds in good health.

100 Percent Yourself

You may have heard people talking about "holistic healing." This is an approach to health based on the belief that all parts of the human body are interconnected and work best when they pull together. To keep yourself well, you need to look after both your mental and physical health. One way to keep stress to a minimum is by trying to achieve a balance in everything you do.

Working hard is important but so are relaxation and leisure activities.

Managing Your Life

Lying beneath a protective layer of bone is possibly one of the most complex structures that the universe has ever known—the brain.

The parietal lobe is concerned with speech and information processing.

The occipital lobe is concerned with aspects of vision.

The cerebellum is concerned with movement, balance, and muscle tone.

The frontal lobe is concerned with planning, reasoning, emotions, and problem solving.

The temporal lobe is concerned with perception, recognition of sounds, and memory.

The brain stem controls breathing, digestion, and heart rate.

Mind Over Matter

Your brain is nothing special to look at and has the texture of warm jello. But it contains more than 100 billion brain cells. It can process millions of bits of information every day and contains your personality, memories, ideas, and thoughts. The main part of the brain is the cerebrum. Its outer, wrinkled layer is made up of millions of brain cells (neurons) and is called the gray matter. This is where most thinking and higher-level brain activities occur.

A Lot of Nerve

A brain cell, or neuron, has two main parts: an axon and the cell body. The axon is a long nerve fiber, which comes from the cell body and carries nerve impulses along it. Each cell body can have thousands of tiny projections, or dendrites, that connect with other neurons. Neurons send messages to one another along the axons at speeds of up to 248 miles (400 km) per hour. The messages cross a tiny gap—the synapse—from an axon to a neighboring dendrite, building up complex web of connections.

DID YOU KNOW?

Your brain is responsible for only about 2.5 percent of your body weight—a tiny amount, given the many important jobs it has to do. However, it uses up about 20 percent of your energy!

Every time you do something, learn something, or think a single thought, neurons connect with one another. It is an extraordinary process that gives you almost unlimited learning potential. There are more potential links between your brain cells than there are atoms in the universe.

Use It or Lose It

Scientists used to believe that neurons only grew in the brains of infants. Now, with the help of new technology, such as functional magnetic resonance imaging (fMRI), scientists have learned that neurons grow throughout life in response to learning.

Experts have also found that there is an explosion of growth and change during puberty. This means that the way you use your brain now will have an enormous impact on how it develops into adulthood. For example, recent research has shown that gray matter grows a lot in young people just before puberty sets in. During puberty, the unused neurons are trimmed away and lost. Does that mean that teens get more stupid? No, it means that teens have an incredible ability to learn.

Research has shown that during puberty, you are more receptive to learning than you are as an adult.

Why? Because it means that the experiences you have at this stage of your life have the ability to permanently alter the way your brain works. Learn how to play an instrument now or learn a new language, and you are creating millions of new neuron connections that will become permanent fixtures in your brain. If you don't attempt to learn new things, or you drink alcohol, you may lose some of your brain's incredible power forever. Misuse of some drugs can also have lasting effects on your brain's development.

FEEL-GOOD FACTOR

Eating omega oils may help your brain develop. These essential oils, such as omega-3 and omega-6, contain lots of DHA, a substance that helps messages zap between brain cells at top speeds. You can get omega oils from oily fish, such as salmon, or some vegetable oils, such as flaxseed and sunflower oils.

Building Brain Power

Now that you know what an incredible organ your brain is, the next thing to learn is how to boost its power so you can reach top performance levels. Eating well and exercising will help, but making the most out of the time you spend learning in school or studying at home will also be rewarding. If you are an effective student, who can learn the most in the shortest amount of time, you will have more opportunities to pursue other interests. In short, it will help you achieve balance in your life.

Learn to Learn

Teachers agree that there are three different learning styles. Most of us have brains that are suited to one or two of the styles:

- Kinesthetic: This style suits learners who need to do, or feel, things to learn. They especially like using their hands.
- Visual: This style suits those who like to see pictures, maps, diagrams, etc.
- Auditory: This style applies to those who learn best by listening and talking.

Kinesthetic people learn better when they can use their hands.

Teachers attempt to use a range of learning materials and methods that appeal to all these styles. Try to identify which learning method suits you best. For example, if you are a visual learner, taking notes in the form of diagrams or webs may work best for you. Kinesthetic learners may find that learning French vocabulary is easier if they practice it while squeezing a ball or walking around the room. Auditory learners could record key facts on their MP3 players and listen to them in the car. The trick is to capitalize on your strengths. There are web sites that can help you test the best way for you to learn. Search for "test your learning style."

MYELINATION

The neurons in a teen's brain undergo a process called myelination. During this process you are better at learning and adapting to new situations, but less likely to control impulses or organize yourself. This process ends in adulthood, when learning and adapting become harder.

Images and diagrams are a good way for visual learners to understand concepts.

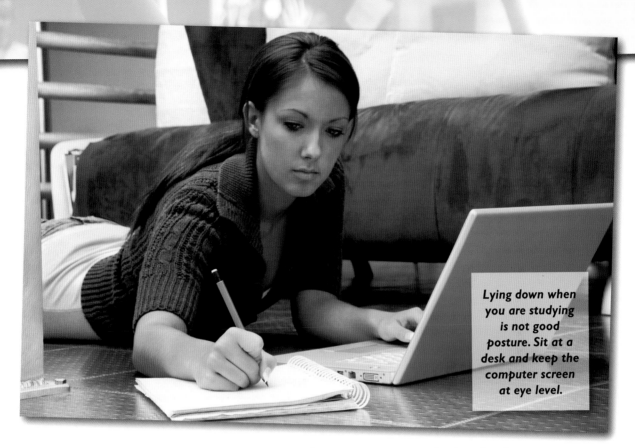

Lying down when you are studying is not good posture. Sit at a desk and keep the computer screen at eye level.

Are You Sitting Comfortably?

The way you hold your body is called posture, and bad posture can lead to back and neck problems. When you are standing and walking, hold yourself straight with your shoulders back. When you are writing, reading, or gaming, make sure your workstation is set up so that you are sitting comfortably and have enough light.

- Position your laptop so you don't bend your neck down to view the screen to see it.

- Using a separate keyboard and mouse may reduce shoulder and wrist strain.
- Relax your eyes every 15 minutes by looking into the distance and refocusing there.
- Get up and move every 20 to 30 minutes. Stretch your arms, rotate your shoulders, and slowly move your head from side to side.
- Avoid junk food, such as candy or chips, while you work. Nuts and seeds make healthier snacks and boost your brain power.

REAL LIFE

"I can't tell you how much I hate homework. But exams—they're okay. When the pressure starts, it's like a switch turns on in my brain. Suddenly, I remember stuff, and my thinking becomes very sharp." David, 16

DID YOU KNOW?

Neuroscientists have found that you are more likely to solve a tricky problem by taking your mind off of it. This allows your brain to explore new connections and find new solutions.

Making the Most of You

Now that you understand how much you can achieve, it's time to work out how to manage your time, exercise, eat right, and get a better night's sleep.

It's okay to spend time with your friends and enjoy extracurricular activities, but remember to set aside time for work.

FEEL-GOOD FACTOR

Write a list of the important things you need to do, putting the most urgent near the top. Check them off as you complete each one. It's a simple, but rewarding, way of getting things done. Keep the list where everyone can see it. The adults in your life will be impressed by your organizational skills!

Manage Your Time

So much to do, so little time. It's a common problem we all have to deal with. One day, you may have to manage a household, look after your own kids, and hold down a job—all at the same time. Learning the skills to manage your time now will help you throughout your life.

1. *Prioritize. This means identifying the most important things to do and putting them first. Homework is probably going to be at the top of your list.*

2. *Focus. Once you have discovered which extracurricular activities you like best, be prepared to focus on just one or two of them.*

3. *Organize. Keep a schedule and try to plan ahead to avoid those last-minute panics. Get backpacks and sports equipment ready the night before.*

4. *Say no. If you have too much to do, then you will have to start turning down some opportunities or activities.*

5. *Ask for help. If you're finding it hard to keep on top of things, ask for help. Avoid a crisis by anticipating problems and asking parents or teachers for advice and support.*

Dealing with Distractions

It can be tough to settle down to study when there are so many distractions. Most young people like to combine some homework with texting, talking on the phone, updating profiles on social-networking sites, and checking e-mails. While it may be true that you can multitask and can focus on all these things at once, try to be honest with yourself. You will probably be able to work best if you concentrate on your studies and allow yourself regular breaks—every 30 minutes or so—to catch up on those other things.

COUCH POTATOES

Recent research has shown that teenagers with TVs in their rooms are more likely to eat junk food, do less homework, exercise less, and are less likely to join in family meals. They watch an average of five hours more TV every week than other teenagers.

In a Virtual World

Gaming can be a lot of fun, and getting totally immersed in a game is half the thrill, but do you make time for more active or social activities? Of course, it's a question of balance.

Why not keep a weekly record of the time you spend on video gaming and watching TV? You may be surprised at how much time you spend on these hobbies. If you start gaming to avoid getting down to the more imporant tasks, such as homework, then you may need to remind yourself of your priorities.

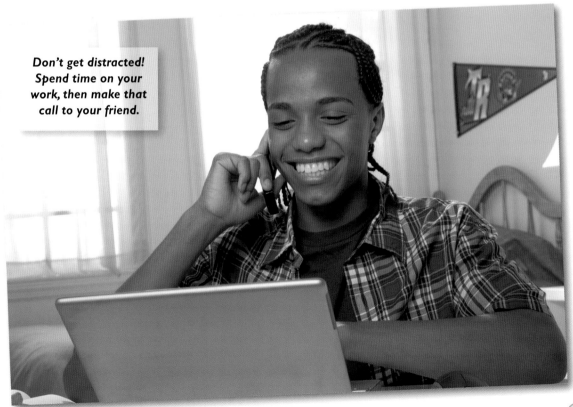

Don't get distracted! Spend time on your work, then make that call to your friend.

Making the Most of You

Body Basics

Doctors recommend that teenagers spend at least one hour a day on physical activity, seven days a week. It doesn't sound like much, but when many young people typically spend up to six hours a day on activities such as watching TV, surfing the Internet, and listening to music, it's easy to see why fitness levels are falling.

There are many benefits to exercising. It improves confidence and self-esteem, builds strong bones and muscles, increases fitness, provides an opportunity to meet new people and—perhaps most importantly—it's fun! If organized team sports don't appeal to you, try to find another way to get active. There are plenty of options: walking to school, yoga classes, skateboarding, and dancing.

There are plenty of ways to keep your body healthy through exercise. Challenge a friend to a game of tennis or go for a jog.

Dump the Junk

You know you shouldn't head for fast food when time is short, but when you only have half an hour between school and football practice, or between your part-time job and going to a movie, what can you do? We all face this problem, but it's especially hard for young adults. You are still growing and you're hungry. These tips may help:

• Be prepared. Keep an emergency supply of fruit, nuts, multigrain energy bars, and smoothies with you.

• Eat well three times a day. Make sure every meal is balanced with a range of filling foods that are low in sugar and fat but high in fiber, fruit, and vegetables.

• Skip soft drinks and sweets— they give you an instant sugar high, but you will feel worse once your body has finished processing these nutritionally light snacks.

Party Food

Taking time out from work to get creative in the kitchen can be very rewarding. Preparing food for your family or friends is a hands-on, fulfilling hobby that enables you to experiment with ingredients and flavors.

Think of cooking as a way to relax, rather than a chore, and you will soon discover that the real joy of food doesn't come from the taste sensation; it is the delight of creating and sharing a meal. Local libraries and book stores stock cookbooks that are ideal for beginners, or you could search for recipes on the Internet.

Vitamins for Vitality

If you eat a balanced diet, you do not need to take supplements. Some of the most important vitamins for good health are:

- Vitamin A is great for the skin and eyes. It is found in eggs, fruits, and vegetables.
- B vitamins are needed for energy and growth. You'll get them from breakfast cereals and whole grain foods.
- Vitamin C fights infections. It is found in fruits and vegetables.
- Vitamin D is essential for bones and teeth. You'll get this in oily fish, dairy products, and eggs. It is also absorbed by the body from sunlight.

Get involved in the cooking! Learning to prepare healthy meals will have long-term benefits as you get older.

Making the Most of You

What's So Special About Sleep?

Sleep is essential for good health. You need it to think clearly, learn, and for memory function. Cut back on your sleep and you are more likely to get into accidents, get depressed, and develop heart disease. During sleep, your body releases a growth hormone—which is especially crucial for teens—and chemicals that fight infections.

Are You Getting Enough Sleep?

Would you be shocked to discover that you should be getting between 9 and 10 hours of sleep every night? That means going to bed no later than 9:00 P.M. so that you can fall asleep by 9:30 P.M. and get up at 7:00 A.M.

Sleep doctors are increasingly concerned about the quality of teens' sleep. Few teens, or their parents, realize how important sleep is. In fact, doctors recommend that people going through puberty should sleep longer and deeper than others. This will give your brain and body a chance to rest and recover from the enormous growth spurt you are going through.

This special colored image shows a brain that has been deprived of sleep. The red areas are the active parts of the brain and the blue are inactive. If you don't get enough sleep, your brain cannot function efficiently.

A good night's sleep is also important in tackling obesity, since sleep-deprived people crave more sweet and starchy foods. Too much sleep, however, quickly disrupts natural sleep patterns and can cause insomnia—the inability to fall asleep.

What Controls Sleep?

The pineal gland is inside the brain. It releases a hormone, melatonin, that controls sleep. The pineal gland is a slave to your body clock. That means your sleep patterns are affected by the amount of daylight. Changing your body clock, by going to bed and getting up at different times, can upset the natural levels of melatonin, making it harder to get to sleep.

Other things can affect your sleep, too. Stimulants, such as caffeine found in tea, coffee, and soda pop, block the effects of sleep hormones. Alcohol is a sedative, which means that it can help you fall asleep more quickly. However, it also disrupts the second half of your night's sleep, causing you to wake up, and disturbing your dreams. Regular alcohol use can lead to sleep deprivation.

SLEEP DEPRIVATION

Most teenagers suffer from sleep deprivation. Melatonin is produced later in the evening in teens, which is why you tend to go to bed later. But you need more sleep than adults and still have to get up for school. Result? Tiredness.

Top Tips for Getting Some Sleep

1. *Avoid caffeinated drinks in the evening, and don't eat just before bedtime.*
2. *Create a routine; doing the same things every evening before bed helps to settle you down.*
3. *Exercise every day.*
4. *Avoid TV, music, or other distractions an hour before you go to bed. Activities stimulate your brain, keeping you awake.*
5. *If worry keeps you from sleeping, address the problem (see page 30).*

Age	Sleep Required (Hours)
6 months	12
10 years	8
15 years	9.5
Adult	8

FEEL-GOOD FACTOR

Recent research has shown that radio waves, generated by your cell phone when you talk into it, can have the same effect as drinking a double espresso, and may delay sleep by up to 30 minutes. If you have problems getting to sleep, it might help to put your phone away!

Avoid watching television in the hour before bed—it stimulates the brain and makes it harder to sleep.

Time for Work

We all have to work. Right now you have homework and exams, but young adults also often have jobs. Juggling work while still finding time to play is a key life skill.

Testing Times

Examinations have been used for centuries to test the knowledge and skills that people have accumulated. In fact, the remains of a diploma recorded on bronze sheets have been found dating from the Roman Empire. It proved that in AD 98 a soldier had acquired key soldiering skills! Tests are a fact of life for most students. The best way to deal with them is to follow a few simple rules.

1. *Be prepared. Make sure you know when and where your exams are scheduled and what you need to know for each one.*

2. *Keep your life in balance. Rest and relaxation, good diet, and exercise are important at exam time.*

3. *Stay motivated. Remind yourself why these exams matter, where success can take you, and the potential consequences of poor performance.*

4. *Study. You have to put in the hours.*

Preparing for Success

A study timetable is an essential tool in preparing for exams. Sticking to it is important, too! If you start studying too early you may get bored. If you wait too long, you could feel overwhelmed by the workload. Calculate how many subjects you need to prepare for, and use your study time accordingly. Organize your time into 30-minute slots, and allow time for breaks.

Studying with friends can help keep you motivated.

Studying hard, but still taking breaks to rest and revive yourself, will lead to success in your exams.

Add other activities, such as sports, jobs and chores, to ensure that you have a balance.

Studying is most effective when you are actively doing something; just reading your notes is not as good as reading sections and rewriting key facts, using bright colors to highlight words or concepts. Diagrams are also a great study aid; they have been proven to significantly improve learning and memory (see page 10).

Reviewing regularly strengthens neural connections. Experts recommend you study and make key notes to begin, then review those notes periodically (in 24 hours, then 7 days, and again in 1 month). This is called a "cascade review" that triggers and strengthens your neural connections.

Setting Goals

Staying motivated can be hard during the time leading up to exams. Make the whole process a little more enjoyable by setting goals and rewarding yourself for meeting them. For example, Adam is 14 and found it hard to start studying geography because he disliked the subject. He learned to break up each subject into small sections, such as weather, ecosystems, and plate tectonics. He rewarded himself with a bike ride or 30 minutes of gaming after he'd studied each one.

Time for Work

The World of Work

Working outside the home has many advantages. It gives you income (money), experience, and key skills. Many universities and colleges prefer students who have shown themselves to be motivated and responsible enough to hold down a job. Jobs can also help you identify possible career paths.

On the downside, jobs will cut into your free time. They can also be tedious, tiring, and difficult. Sometimes they involve working late, which can reduce your ability to study. It is important to find a job where the pros outweigh the cons. If work is affecting your studies, consider finding another way to earn money, and discuss the situation with your parents or school counselor.

Preparing a good résumé is the first step toward getting a job.

Finding a Job

Identify the places you would like to work. Visit them with a copy of your résumé, making sure you look clean and neat. A résumé lists your references and any work experience you have. Include information about responsible positions you have held at school, such as being a member of the school council or a team captain. Include a short personal statement outlining your key qualities.

If you are invited for an interview, follow these simple rules for success:

- Dress appropriately and arrive on time.
- Shake hands firmly and look the interviewer in the eyes. Smile!
- Answer the questions with honesty. Share your good qualities and relevant experience.
- Always have a couple of questions prepared to show how knowledgeable you are.
- Thank the interviewer for his or her time, and ask when you can expect to hear back.

DID YOU KNOW?

There are laws that govern the type of work young people can do and the number of hours they are permitted to work. Individual states also set minimum wages. Check the laws that apply to you before you take on a job.

FEEL-GOOD FACTOR

Find out what the health and safety regulations are for the job that you do. Make sure you follow the rules, and never put yourself in any type of danger, no matter what an employer tells you to do.

Juggling a Job

Taking on a job with regular hours will make it easier for you to maintain your study plans. You will soon learn which parts of your life must change to make way for your new responsibility. If necessary, be prepared to give up, or cut down on, some of your leisure activities.

If your job has irregular working hours, then you'll have to be more organized. Put your schedules on the family bulletin board, so that everyone in the family knows where you are going to be and when. This will also help you become a reliable and punctual employee.

Whether you work in a store or take on a paper route, be organized and professional about your work.

Time to Move On

When you decide to leave a job, it is polite—and sensible—to follow the proper protocol. You will be expected to give notice, which means giving your employer a reasonable time to replace you. A week's notice should be the minimum. Assuming you are leaving on good terms, you should ask your employer for a reference. It should give the dates you were employed, your position, and a brief outline of your duties. It should also include positive comments about how well you performed these duties. This reference will help you find new work.

Make a good impression in a job interview by dressing neatly and shaking hands.

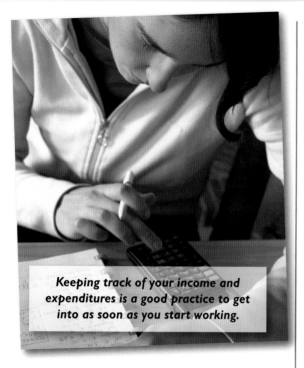

Keeping track of your income and expenditures is a good practice to get into as soon as you start working.

Money Matters

Oscar Wilde once said, "When I was young I thought money was the most important thing in life; now I'm old I know that it is." Many people would disagree that money is the most important thing in life, but there's no doubt that having some money is usually better than having none. Controlling your own income and expenditures are important parts of preparing for adulthood, so it helps to have some pointers for making the most of your money.

Credit cards let you buy things without having to pay immediately. With a debit card, the money comes out of your account right away.

Balancing a Budget

A budget is a money plan. It lists all the money you receive and all the money you spend. A budget is also a planning tool, so you could use it to track the amount of income you expect to get along with the amount you expect to spend. The difference between the two will be your profit or loss. To avoid a loss, and therefore a debt, you have to balance your budget by either finding other ways to make money or by coming up with ideas to cut back on your spending.

UNDERSTANDING MONEY

Money matters can be confusing, partly because of the vocabulary. Money terms include:

Debt. This is money you owe to the bank or to someone else.

Income. This is money you receive, such as earnings and allowance/pocket money.

Inflation. This is the way the value of money tends to fall over time, which increases the cost of things.

Interest. This is money paid to you in return for leaving your money in a savings account. You also pay interest on a debt.

Loan. This is money the bank lends you; you'll be charged interest.

Tax. This is money people have to pay to the government when they have a job.

Mark Zuckerberg set up Facebook while he was still a teenager.

Making Money

The simplest way to make money is ideal for the lazy; just put whatever you have into a savings account and leave it there. If the bank is able to offer you a good rate of interest, you will make some money. If the current rate of inflation is high, though, any extra money you make could be wiped out by higher prices. Nevertheless, saving money is a great habit to get into, and it means you'll always have an emergency fund when you need it.

Earning money is more difficult, of course. Most teenagers opt for jobs to supplement any allowance they receive, but a few show an extraordinary flair for innovation and business enterprise. Mark Zuckerberg, for example, was a 19-year-old college student when he launched Facebook. Now he's one of the world's richest men.

Saving Money

Cutting back on what you spend can be tough, because it means doing without things you really want. Welcome to the world of adults! Decide which costs are essential and which are more of a luxury to determine where you can start saving.

REAL LIFE

"I had a paper route for three years and saved enough money to buy all the gadgets I need to record and edit videos. I now post them on the Internet and make money from advertising revenue. I still do my paper route, because I'm saving for college." Josh, 17

Choices and Changes

You have many choices to make—about love, your social life, exams, work, and a lot more—but you may still be struggling to find out who you are and what you want.

People who are risk takers are much more likely to threaten their health by experimenting with drugs or alcohol than those who are more cautious.

decision for him. He is liberated from the agony of making choices, but without a moral framework helping him to weigh the reasons for every choice, his life descends into tragedy and lawlessness.

The story illustrates how important good decision making is and shows that we all have to bear both moral and practical responsibility for the outcomes of our choices. Throwing dice relies on luck and is the coward's way. Good decision making takes wisdom and courage.

A Roll of the Dice

The Dice Man, a novel by Luke Rhinehart, was published in the 1970's and became a cult classic. The story tells of a psychiatrist who wants to let the roll of the dice settle every

FEEL-GOOD FACTOR

Dopamine is a brain chemical that makes you feel good. Your body makes more dopamine when you take dangerous risks, like driving very fast. But it also produces dopamine when you try new things, play sports, and challenge yourself in positive ways.

What's the Risk?

One of the hardest things about making choices and decisions is that you have to take some risks; few outcomes are ever guaranteed. Better decisions are made when you have taken steps to minimize the risk of a bad outcome. That means:

• Taking time

• Weighing the evidence

• Considering all possible outcomes

Does that process sound typical of the teenagers you know? Of course not! One of the most exciting things about adolescence is that it is a time of excitement, spontaneity, innovation, and risk taking.

A LONGER LIFE

People who are risk takers are 10 times more likely to take drugs than people who are more cautious. Young people are more likely to take risks, which partially explains why nearly half of new HIV/AIDS cases occur in people under the age of 25.

In Two Minds

Risk may be about danger, but it is also about opportunity. Young people are usually more open to new ideas and experiences, but the flip side to this positive attribute is that you may be more prone to taking dangerous chances. No one knows for sure why teenagers tend to take more risks than children or adults, but here are two possible reasons:

1. *During our evolution, it suited the human race to have young people who were risk takers, who sought new environments and food sources for their families, and who were willing to confront danger.*
2. *Young people simply lack the wisdom and experience to be able to make sound judgments, but they will learn as they mature.*

You can benefit from the experiences of your parents, guardians, and teachers. Listen to the advice they offer. You can choose not to follow it, but it makes sense to equip yourself with all the information you need to make good choices.

DID YOU KNOW?

Most teenagers do not use drugs. Most adolesents under the age of 16 do not get drunk regularly, and have never had sex.

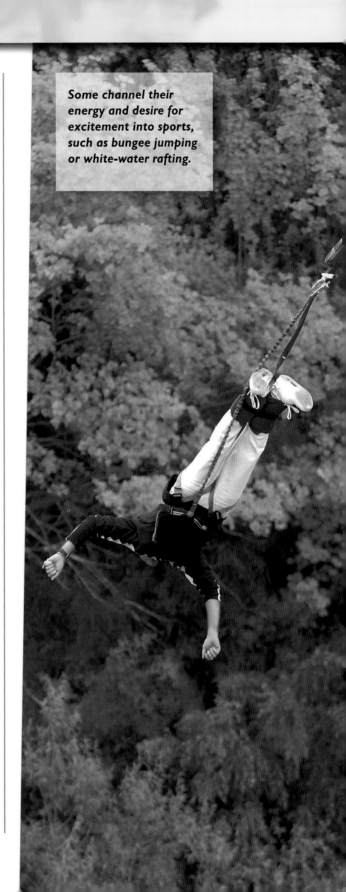

Some channel their energy and desire for excitement into sports, such as bungee jumping or white-water rafting.

Choices and Changes

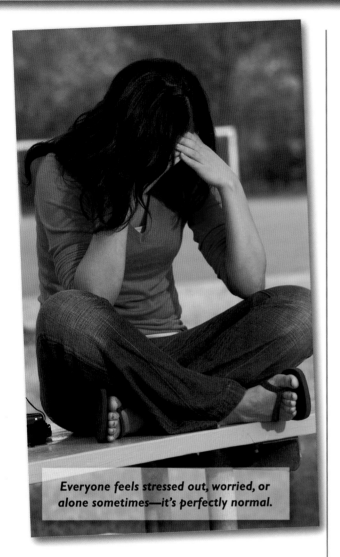

Everyone feels stressed out, worried, or alone sometimes—it's perfectly normal.

REAL LIFE

"My best friend Paul started acting all weird, ignoring me, not going out and stuff. So I dropped him. Turned out he was depressed because his dad was very ill. I felt bad because I didn't help him. We talk about it now, and I try to be there for him."

Dan, 14

All Change

Adolescence is a time of enormous, all-consuming change. Like the transition from caterpillar to butterfly, you are undergoing a metamorphosis. There may be times when the physical, mental, and spiritual changes you are experiencing become very painful and frightening. There may be other times when you feel as if you are a steady sailboat, trying to carve its way through a sea of turmoil. It is worth remembering that your friends are likely to be dealing with changes, too. They can offer you advice, or they may benefit from your support.

Body Blues

During puberty, your body changes day by day. Teenagers often feel worried about these changes, and wonder whether they are "normal." The truth is that everyone starts and finishes puberty at a different time and progresses through it in a different way. There is no "normal" when it comes to bodies. However, feeling a bit scared or insecure about these changes is normal. If you feel anxious about any aspect of how your body is changing, you can discuss it with your doctor in confidence.

When you're a teenager, hormones can send your emotions all over the place, making you feel stressed.

Rocky Waters

Everybody, young or old, is more likely to thrive and feel happy if their home life is settled and secure, and they feel loved. Sometimes those circumstances do not exist, though. Here are just some of the stressful situations you may have experienced or that you may worry about:

the signs of anxiety and stress, and acquiring the skills to help you control them, will help you now and in the future.

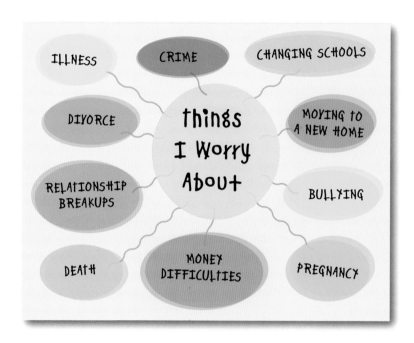

ILLNESS
CRIME
CHANGING SCHOOLS
DIVORCE
things I Worry About
MOVING TO A NEW HOME
RELATIONSHIP BREAKUPS
BULLYING
DEATH
MONEY DIFFICULTIES
PREGNANCY

When we cannot control our environment and the changes that are being forced upon us, we feel very anxious. As you move toward adulthood, you will be more affected by circumstances that your parents were once able to protect you from. Learning how to recognize

The Ups and Downs of Hormones

Hormones are responsible for many things. During adolescence, the sex hormones, estrogen and testosterone, are not just causing lots of changes in your physical appearance; they are battling it out in your brain, too.

The levels of hormones in your blood are unstable, peaking and dropping in an unpredictable manner. This can cause mood swings, higher levels of aggression and anger, and depression. On the plus side, these chemical messengers are one of the reasons you can fall in love and excel in sports. They also help you develop an adult brain, capable of making good judgments, planning a work schedule, and—one day—caring for a family of your own.

FEEL-GOOD FACTOR

Try not to bottle up your feelings. When the prospect of change is making you feel anxious, you will feel better if you talk about your concerns. Talking may help you identify what you most fear and help you find practical solutions.

Bullying is one of many situations that can cause you stress during your teenage years.

Under Pressure

There are times in everyone's life when pressure builds up, and we feel very stressed. Recognizing stress is the first step toward learning how to deal with it—and preventing it.

If you're under pressure, it can affect your sleep patterns and leave you awake and worried throughout the night.

the danger or flee from it (this is called the "fight or flight" reaction). Your heart beats faster and the stress hormones, adrenalin and cortisol, race through your bloodstream. You become more alert, focused, energetic, and responsive to situations.

So stress can work positively to keep you from danger and help you perform better in challenging situations. Unfortunately, if you are stressed for a long time, it can have a negative impact, affecting your mental and physical well-being. Stress can:

- Make you feel more pain.
- Give you digestive problems.
- Damage your heart.
- Reduce your immunity to illness.
- Affect sleep.
- Lead to depression.

What Is Stress?

Stress is your body's natural response to a bad situation. If your life is no longer balanced, you are feeling threatened, anxious, or overwhelmed, and your body may react with stress.

Stress is your body's way of protecting you from danger. When you feel threatened, your body tries to prepare you to confront

SYMPTOMS OF STRESS

Check out these signs to see if you might be suffering from the symptoms of stress:

- *Tiredness*
- *Crying*
- *Loss of appetite*
- *Sleeplessness*
- *Compulsive behavior*
- *Feelings of alarm*
- *Use of drugs and alcohol*

Why Me?

Have you noticed how some people are able to remain very calm when others become agitated and tense? Everyone deals with stress differently due to genetics, the examples set by our families, the environment, and attitudes.

Scientists have found males are more likely to suffer poor health as a result of stress than females, and adolescents who belong to a religious faith are often able to cope better with stress. This may be because they have more friends and strong social networks. Even caring for a pet can reduce your heart rate and blood pressure!

Life on the Edge

Stress and anger management issues are just two of a range of problems that many teens have to deal with. The flurry of emotions, physical changes, experiences at home and school, and hormonal instability—all associated with

FEEL-GOOD FACTOR

Huge growth spurts in the brain are associated with extremes of emotion. It is no wonder that both toddlers and teenagers are prone to tears and tantrums! Unlike a toddler, you can probably control yourself. Take a deep breath...

adolescence—can lead to an imbalance in mental health.

Teens who suffer this type of imbalance may develop problems such as phobias (irrational fears), eating disorders, and obsessive-compulsive disorders (OCDs). The worst-affected young adults may resort to self harm, become very depressed, and even suicidal.

These are problems you cannot solve by yourself and usually get worse if they are not treated. If you are suffering from any of these problems, it is important to find an adult that you trust and are comfortable with so you can speak to them and get help.

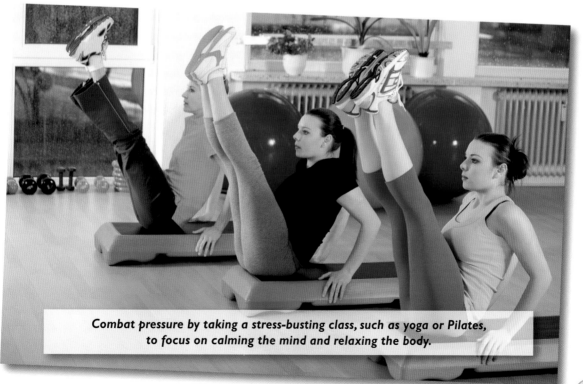

Combat pressure by taking a stress-busting class, such as yoga or Pilates, to focus on calming the mind and relaxing the body.

Dealing with Stress

It is possible to deal with the negative effects of stress and find ways to reduce or prevent it. First, identify the type of stress you suffer from:

1. *Rational. Some stress is brought on by rational factors: you don't have enough time to do your work, you have a large debt, you have upset a close friend. Rational stress can be tackled by having an organized, problem-solving attitude.*

REAL LIFE

"At exam time I feel as if I've got a squirming cat in my belly. Sometimes I get so nervous I am physically sick. It doesn't matter if my teachers tell me an exam isn't that important – it is to me."

Li San, 16

2. *Irrational. Some stress is brought on by irrational fears: the house will burn down, my parents will die, or no one likes me. Irrational stress is harder to deal with. It may be brought about by low self-esteem or an unrealistic understanding of situations. Counseling often helps people who are stressed for irrational reasons.*

Surfing the Stress

How can you manage your stress?

1. *Prioritize it. Stress often comes from having too many things to do, or too many problems to deal with. Refer to page 12 and the section on managing time.*
2. *Solve it. Write a list of all the things that make you feel anxious. Choose one problem and identify a solution. Try to find a possible solution for all the problems on your list.*
3. *Cool it. Try to change your reaction to stressful situations. Practice slow breathing and relaxing your muscles. Try to turn anger into irritation, hate to dislike, etc.*
4. *Avoid it. If certain situations always make you stressed, see if you can avoid or change them.*
5. *Heal it. Stress is a physical reaction, so deal with the impact it's having on your body by looking after your health. Keep fit and well fed, take long walks, and spend time with friends or pursuing your hobbies. Even petting a cat or walking the dog can help reduce stress. Consider taking up stress-busting classes, such as art or yoga.*

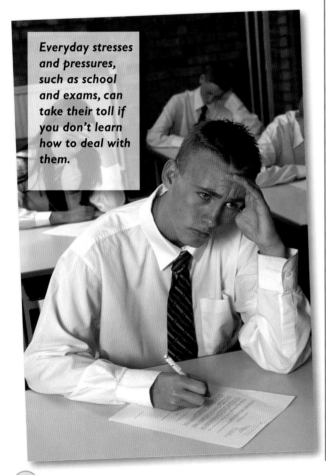

Everyday stresses and pressures, such as school and exams, can take their toll if you don't learn how to deal with them.

Sports and hobbies are an important way of relieving pressure. It's important to make time for fun.

Keep Your Cool

Children and teenagers sometimes find it hard to control anger, and violent rages may result. Boys are more likely to have problems managing their anger than girls. Most doctors agree that anger is usually a symptom of another feeling, such as rejection, frustration, or failure. If you get angry or violent, these suggestions may help you:

1. *Recognize the triggers that make you lose control, and take steps to avoid them.*
2. *Work out which things are valid reasons for getting angry (someone hits you), and which ones are not (someone ignores you).*
3. *Get organized. One of the main triggers for anger is poor time management. Is your life in balance?*
4. *Talk, talk, and talk. It will help you find out why you are angry and what you could do about it in a more constructive way.*

FEEL-GOOD FACTOR

Sports and hobbies make a huge difference in how you cope with the stressful parts of your life. Make time for these activities, but don't use them to delay doing other things that need to be done. After one hour of gaming, that essay will still be waiting for you.

The Best You Can Be

A few years ago, you probably knew exactly who you were and what you wanted. With adolescence, that changes. You are developing an adult "sense of self."

Magazines can give you the impression that you have to be model-thin to be attractive, but this isn't true.

What Is Self-Esteem?

Self-esteem is a confidence in your abilities and worth. Teenagers often experience a drop in their self-esteem. It can be hard to determine who you are when your body, and your feelings, are constantly changing.

Young adults often feel a strong urge to belong to a group—to conform, or fit in. This pressure to feel accepted can make you even more conscious of your identity. The programs you watch on TV, the magazines you read, and the way adults make you feel, can also affect your self-esteem.

DID YOU KNOW?

Research has shown that adolescents who suffer from low self-esteem are more likely to take up smoking or have underage sex than those with more confidence.

You in the Mix

People with low self-esteem may suffer a greater imbalance in their lives than their more confident peers. If you have a poor sense of your value, you may be reluctant to make friends, socialize in groups, or get involved in sports. You might find it more frightening to seek out new experiences, or you may feel depressed. These are just some of the important reasons for improving your self-esteem. Boost your feelings of worth by following these suggestions:

1. *Cut out negative thoughts. It may sound simplistic, but it works. Every time a negative thought about yourself pops into your mind, replace it with a positive one. Every day, write down at least three things you like about yourself.*
2. *Be realistic. Look around you—how many people are perfect in body and mind? No one is. Our flaws make us human and unique.*
3. *Put a positive spin on it. Okay, so you made a mistake; treat it as an opportunity to learn, and don't make the same mistake again.*
4. *Get out there. Try new things, start a new hobby, set goals, and find time to help people in need.*

Finding your own style is good—just make sure you're being true to yourself and not just following a trend so that you "fit in."

Finding Yourself

Young people who are trying to find out who they are demonstrate their inner turmoil in a variety of ways. You may recognize them:

- Status symbols—do you feel pressure to wear the "right" clothes or shoes, own state-of-the-art technology, or flash your cash?
- Hero worship—while looking for a role in life, many teens want to be like certain celebrities or musicians.

FEEL-GOOD FACTOR

Write a list of 10 qualities that you admire and respect, such as honesty and humor. The list will help you identify the type of person you are or want to be. Do your friends have some of these qualities? If not, what qualities do they have that you like?

- Rule breaking—acts of rebellion show that you are separating from your parents, while pleasing your peers.
- Acting older— engaging in activities that are associated with adults, such as smoking, drinking, and sex, make adolescents feel mature.
- Forming groups— belonging to a group can give you a powerful sense of belonging, social status, and a group identity.

The Best You Can Be

Making Connections

Communication is the way we exchange information to increase understanding. There are many parts of your brain that work together when you communicate. Neuroscientists have discovered that, because the brains of adolescents are developing and growing, there can be a change in the way teens are able to communicate. This can lead to misunderstandings and even a breakdown in family relationships.

Blushing is a form of communication that we are unable to control, so it makes us feel very vulnerable. It tells people about possible emotions we may be experiencing.

Body language speaks volumes. When teenagers slouch, adults often think they're being sulky or rude.

Body Talk

Talking is one of the most obvious ways we can communicate, but we also use our body language to show how we are feeling. This is called nonverbal communication, and it is one area where teenagers often struggle. They may misread other people's body language or give out misleading signals to those around them.

Teens with low self-esteem, for example, may hunch their shoulders and hide their eyes behind their hair. Adults often read this body language as sulkiness, rudeness, or a lack of interest. On the other hand, children between the ages of 11 and 12 lose their ability to read faces and understand other people's emotions. They don't recover this essential skill until they are in their late teens.

RED IN THE FACE

We blush when we feel strong emotions, such as anger, guilt, and embarrassment. People who are shy or more anxious about other people's opinions of them blush more easily. Thankfully, it is something most of us grow out of as we become more confident.

Empathy—the Emotion of Understanding

Someone with empathy is able to share and understand someone else's feelings. Thanks to the way your brain is developing at the moment, it is quite likely that you do not score very highly on empathy skills.

Scientists have learned that the brains of teens and adults reacted differently when they were asked to deal with situations where empathy would help. It was found that adults used the parts of their brains that enabled them to imagine how their actions would affect other people's feelings. These parts of teen brains barely flickered into life!

The good news is that empathy does develop. By the time you are an adult, you will be much more sensitive to other people's feelings. In the meantime, try these tips:

- Ask: If you are not sure what someone is feeling, just ask!
- Hear: Listen to what people are telling you, and look at their body language at the same time.
- Imagine: How would you feel in the same situation?

Move Like You Mean It

When you are not feeling confident—at school, work, or in a social situation—you can fool people into thinking you are. Think about what message your body language is giving out, and adapt it if necessary.

- Stand tall—you will gain height and look more powerful. Holding your head high indicates self-esteem.
- Hands free—don't wrap your arms around your body; people will think you are unfriendly. Try not to touch your face, as this signals self-consciousness.
- Eye to eye—look people in the eye when you meet them, and hold their gaze when you talk, or listen, to them. This is one of the most powerful and engaging ways of communicating.

President Bill Clinton was a popular politician, known for his communication skills and ability to maintain eye contact.

The Best You Can Be

Uniquely You

How would you describe yourself? Are you outgoing, funny, attractive? Maybe you are intelligent, caring, or shy? We all have an idea about what makes us unique—and the way we spend our time in work and play also helps to define us. So, you may also think of yourself as a good student, a football player, an animal lover, a chess player, a singer, or an artist.

Hopefully, if you enjoy a well-balanced life, you will be able to think of a range of words to describe yourself. For some people, the list may be much shorter and limited to a single word or term, such as disabled, gay, dyslexic, autistic, caring, gifted, talented, foreign, orphan, bullied, elite athlete, bereaved, poor, ethnic minority, wealthy, or homeless.

Made from a Different Mold

Sometimes the things that identify us are used to define us. They can become barriers to new experiences, friendships, and activities. During the teen years, when there is pressure to fit in with a crowd and a need to begin separating from the adults in your life, it can be particularly hard to be different. It doesn't matter whether the difference is one that you were born with or one that has come about as a result of circumstance—it still hurts.

If the people around you have a one-dimensional view of your identity, abilities, and attitudes, it can be exasperating to try to make them see the real you. Challenging people's preconceptions about you can become a lifetime of work.

DID YOU KNOW?

Gay and lesbian young people are more likely to suffer depression, suicidal feelings, and academic failure because of low self-esteem caused by abuse, bullying, and discrimination.

The most important thing, however, is that you keep challenging yourself to make the most of your strengths and refuse to be defined by your differences or difficulties.

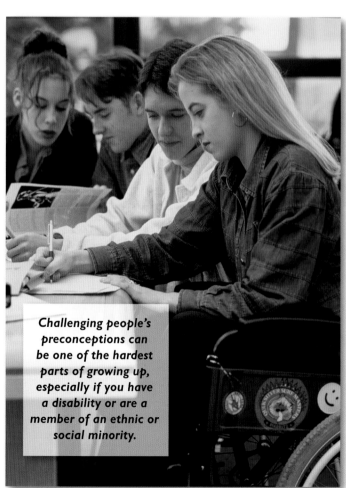

Challenging people's preconceptions can be one of the hardest parts of growing up, especially if you have a disability or are a member of an ethnic or social minority.

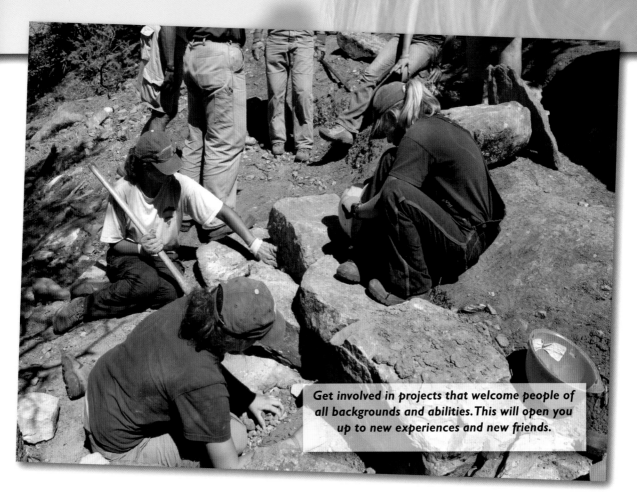

Get involved in projects that welcome people of all backgrounds and abilities. This will open you up to new experiences and new friends.

Finding a Balance

Whatever your circumstances, you are entitled to enjoy a good education, a loving home life, the chance to exercise and relax, and to have opportunities to spend time with other young people. If you feel that you are being denied or deprived of these basic rights then it's time to ask for help. Parents, teachers, school counselors, social workers, and organizations that work with young people are all obliged to ensure that every child and young person is able to both work and play in a safe and happy environment.

FEEL-GOOD FACTOR

Join groups or activities where you can meet other young people with similar interests, backgrounds, or problems. You will find support, friendship, and a sense of belonging that you may not find elsewhere.

CHILDREN'S RIGHTS

The 1990 UN Convention on the Rights of the Child states no child should be discriminated against. All children under 18 have a right to protection and development and the right to contribute toward decisions that affect them.

Friends and Family

As family bonds loosen, you will find that people of the same age become some of the most important influences in your life. Balancing family and social relationships can be difficult, but there are ways of getting it right.

Friendships

Friends can help you deal with the demands of work and get the most from your downtime. They are easy to talk to because they are probably going through the same changes and experiences.

For many teens, friendships matter more than almost anything else, which can cause imbalance in their life. Devoting all your time to your friends could mean that your studies suffer or that you don't have time to concentrate on your other interests. Thanks to the Internet and cell phones, you can now find out exactly what your friends are doing at any time—and they know everything about you.

Good Friends, Bad Friends

Good friends offer you support, listen to your problems, and respect you —but it is a two-way street. Being loyal, kind, and attentive to your friends will help these relationships to grow and to last.

Real friends are there to support you any time you need them. Know the difference between true friends and "fair-weather friends."

Some friends fall short of the mark; they may expect you to drop everything so that you can spend time with them. They may be kind one day, cruel the next. Fickle friends ignore you when someone "better" comes along. You end up feeling used and lonely. People who try to force you to do things you don't want to do are not real friends. Choosing how to make good friends is a life skill. So is learning not to waste your time on the ones who keep hurting you.

Groups and Gangs

When you belong to a group of friends, you feel secure, protected, and accepted. Sometimes, however, a group begins to exert a cruel type of power. When this happens, it has transformed into a gang and you should avoid it.

How to Recognize a Gang

- Gang members are expected to behave a certain way—there may be an unwritten set of "rules" for all members.

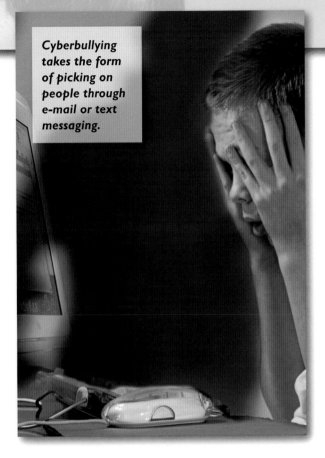

Cyberbullying takes the form of picking on people through e-mail or text messaging.

- Gangs are exclusive. Members of a gang like to make themselves look, sound, or behave differently than others.
- Gang members make themselves feel better by hurting people outside the gang. This is bullying.

Bullying

Bullying is behavior that hurts other people. It includes name-calling, physical threats and attacks, stealing or damaging your belongings, spreading rumors and lies, and turning other people against you. Most people who bully have a low sense of self-esteem; they make themselves feel better by hurting others. Many people who bully have been bullied themselves.

Cyberbullying is relatively new. It involves bullying on the Internet—often on social networking sites—sending insulting or intimidating texts, silent phone calls, and nasty instant messages.

If you are a victim of any form of bullying, you must seek help from an adult. Parents and teachers will support you, and the police have the technology to track down cyberbullies.

FEEL-GOOD FACTOR

Beat the bullies by pretending that their taunts or actions don't affect you. Make it clear that you don't value their opinion anyway, and they might just leave you alone.

Friends and Family

Adults Grow Up, Too

While you are carving a new path through life, the adults around you are trying to adjust to the new, ever-changing you. They know you are growing up and becoming independent and are trying to help you in the process. As they let go, the balance of their lives shifts dramatically.

For many parents, this time can be traumatic, stressful, and frightening. Since the day you were born, they have had an enormous responsibility: looking after you. Don't be surprised that they still take that responsibility seriously and find this time of transition as difficult as you do.

Many teenagers feel like running away from home at some point, but there's always a better solution than life on the streets.

Bridging the Divide

You may feel that a chasm is opening up between you and your parents, which will only get worse the more time you spend away from them. Maintaining good balance in your life includes being with your family. When you plan your week, consider setting aside time to be with your parents and siblings.

Communication and trust are two important parts of the teen and parent relationship. Your parents need to know that you can behave responsibly, are reliable, and that you are being honest with them. Keeping the lines of communication open will build trust; talking through problems or disagreements is more likely to get positive results than shouting and slamming doors. Here are some tips for getting along with your parents:

- Volunteer information about where you are going and who you are seeing, before being asked.
- Ask them for advice. Even if you don't take it, they'll be flattered.
- Empathize and show you care about their feelings.
- Do something helpful without being asked.
- Say something nice.

What a Chore!

One common reason that teens and their parents argue is because of chores. It would be perfectly normal for you to put chores way down on your list of priorities. But if you want to help keep the peace at home, you should consider putting chores higher up on your list!

Your parents want you to do your fair share of work around the house—and that's a reasonable expectation. They also want you to learn how to cook and clean, because when you leave home you will have to be able to do these things for yourself. There's no getting away from it, chores are dull, but they have to be done. Doing them without moaning will earn your parents' respect. Do extra chores, and you may be able to negotiate a bigger allowance or a later curfew.

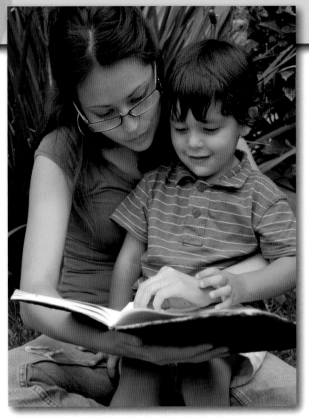

Prove you can be trusted by helping out with younger brothers or sisters.

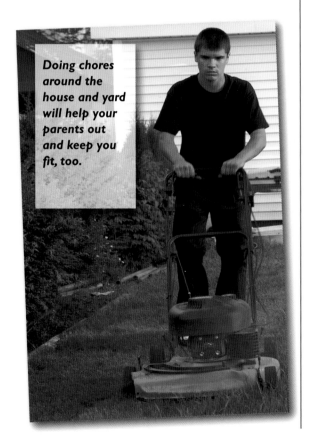

Doing chores around the house and yard will help your parents out and keep you fit, too.

Parent Problems

As we grow up, we realize that adults are not perfect—they can make mistakes, too. Some adults, however, fall far short of what you have a right to expect from them. If poor parenting or abusive relationships of any type are harming you and your development, you should seek help. Speak to adults you can trust about these problems.

FEEL-GOOD FACTOR

Turn a "no" into a "maybe": instead of saying, "Can I do X?" ask, "When would I be allowed to do X"? It often works!

A Bright Future

Growing up is about so much more than the physical signs of change—it is about maturing, taking responsibility, and making choices about your daily life and future.

Open Doors

During your teens, you are still a work in progress: many doors are open to you. You can learn new things, change your outlook, and opinions. Even your ability to understand and communicate complex issues improves with age.

In the past, your life was organized by your parents and school; now that's changing and it's up to you where your journey takes you. Using tools that help you build balance in your life—and reach equilibrium—will help you emerge from adolescence with a healthy body and mind.

REAL LIFE

"I loved being a teenager, but not all the time. Everything was either wonderful or terrible. I feel much more settled now. Those extremes were good, but only for a short while." Hannah, 22

Key Skills for a Balanced Life

- Prioritizing your life. Remind yourself of the important things that need to be done. Check that time for your studies, family, friends, and leisure activities feature in your priorities.
- Planning a future. Working today is easier when you can imagine where it may lead. Think about what career you would like, and find out what you need to achieve to get there.
- Managing time. Writing lists, plans, and timetables can help you manage your time

All the skills you're learning now are preparing you for your career and your life ahead. Enjoy it!

effectively—and get much more out of your life. Set goals that you need to reach within a certain time.

- Avoiding distractions. Wasting time is easy, but it won't get you any nearer to your goals. Remind yourself of your priorities, and exert some self-control.
- Discussing problems. Communication is the best way to start dealing with problems. If talking to your parents is hard, you could write a letter to them.
- Resting and relaxing. These parts of your life matter just as much as work. Finding time to relax or play is just as important as making time for studying.

Make It Happen

Follow these five simple steps to stay on the path to success.

1. *Connect. Be sociable and spend time with other people, either working or playing. Be sure to make eye contact with people when you talk to them. Keep the lines of communication open between yourself and your family.*
2. *Be active. Enjoy the fresh air. Exercise your body and benefit mentally and physically.*
3. *Enjoy. Stop and savor the special moments and the good times. Be aware of what is precious and good in your world, and take time to appreciate those many things.*
4. *Challenge. Remember that your developing brain craves learning and new, positive experiences so that it can grow to its potential.*
5. *Give. Sharing and caring help us to gain a more realistic perspective of our own problems and make us feel good. From giving a compliment to giving your time, small acts of kindness are good for your inner self and the people whose lives you touch.*

Becoming an adult means learning how to care and share. Get out there, challenge yourself, and help others in the process.

YOU'RE NOT ALONE

It is important to know that you are not alone; everyone goes through adolescence. Many people have experienced the difficulties that you are facing. Talking to friends, teachers, and family can help. There are also organizations that can help you deal with specific problems or goals.

Glossary

adolescence the time of development between the beginning of puberty and adulthood

anxiety a feeling of worry or tension

blood pressure the force that blood exerts on the walls of the blood vessels. Blood pressure can vary according to age and general health

body clock an internal timekeeper that controls some of your body's functions

counseling a service that offers advice and support for people on a range of issues

dehydrated when the body does not have enough fluids in it

depression an emotional state of gloom and deep sadness or a medical condition characterized by the same emotions

discrimination unfair treatment of a person, often because of their race, religion, or sex

empathy the power to imagine and understand someone else's feelings

estrogen the female hormone that controls puberty and some parts of the reproductive system

expenditure the amount of money you spend

gene a section of DNA that carries a particular inherited characteristic, such as body shape

genetics the study of genes and inheritance

heart disease a narrowing or blockage of the blood vessels that provide oxygen-rich blood to the heart

hormones chemical messengers produced by glands in the body; hormones are transported by the blood to instruct cells and organs to work in a particular way

irrational not logical, not following reason or good sense

melatonin the hormone that brings on sleep

menstruate when the lining of the uterus passes from the body; known as a period

metamorphosis a complete change of body form

myelination the process of adding a myelin (fatty) layer to a neuron so that it can transmit electrical impulses more quickly

neuroscientist a scientist who studies the nervous system, especially the brain

obesity when a person has an abnormally high amount of body fat

preconception having a belief about something before knowing the facts

protocol an accepted code of behavior

psychiatrist a doctor who specializes in treating mental health problems

puberty the period during which adolescents reach sexual maturity and are capable of reproduction

rational logical or reasonable

sedative something that calms you down

stress an emotional feeling of strain, tension, or anxiety, and a physical state of the body

supplements pills or liquids taken to add nutrients, such as vitamins, to the diet

testosterone the sex hormone that controls some aspects of male puberty and the male reproductive system

vitamin a substance that is essential, in very small amounts, for health

yoga a type of exercise that aims to bring peace and awareness through mental and physical exercises

Further Information

Books

The Anxiety Workbook for Teens:
Activities to Help You Deal with Anxiety and Worry
by Lisa M. Schab
(Instant Help Publications, 2008)

Blame My Brain
by Nicola Morgan
(Walker Books, 2007)

The Teen Brain
by Sherre Florence Phillips
(Chelsea House, 2007)

Stressed Out Students' Guide to Managing Your Time
by Lisa Medoff
(Kaplan Pub, 2009)

Teen Success: Ideas to Move Your Mind
by Beatrice J. Elye
(Great Potential Press, 2007)

Where's My Stuff?
by Samantha Moss
(Zest Books, 2007)

Web Sites

http://www.teenshealth.org
Information and advice about food and fitness.

http://www.girlshealth.gov
Just for girls—your body, emotions, relationships,
safety, growing up, and more.

http://www.osha.gov/SLTC/teenworkers/
teenworkers.html
Information on protecting teen health by
promoting safe work experiences.

http://www.teengrowth.com
Resources for fitness, nutrition, bullying, family,
friends, and school.

Index